CRYOUT SERIES

I0165030

I KNOW YOUR WORKS

'BOLA OLU-JORDAN

I KNOW YOUR WORKS

Copyright © 2013 'Bola Olu-Jordan

ISBN: 978-50377-3-8
ISBN-13:978-978-5037739

This edition is published by CRYOUT Publications for worldwide distribution. For more information on foreign distribution or translation, please, visit our internet site at www.cryoutreach.com

All Scripture quotations, unless otherwise indicated are taken from the Holy Bible, New King James Version. © 1982 by Thomas Nelson, Inc. Used by permission. All rights reserved. please, note that CRYOUT Publications' publishing style capitalizes certain pronouns in Scripture that refer to the Father, Son, and Holy Spirit, and may differ from other publisher's style.

Published by CRYOUT Publications
Africa. Florida. Edmonton

Printed in the United States of America

DEDICATION

To David Sheats and Anibal Velez.

CONTENTS

PREFACE

In an age where the word of God is scarce and the way of God is narrow, standards are lowered to 'recruit' people into the kingdom.

Often, this is through a seeming orchestrated conversion to Christianity without a relationship with Jesus. People are brought in through a sincere deception that God is desperate to have them in His kingdom. He is also willing to gratify as many as will come with benefits and shower them with miracles.

That sounds much like the acts of the last days church. It is the 'Christianity' they are introduced to and the faith they practice and propagate. As long as there are people who act better than the worst of all, they are qualified. And with a little commitment and membership spirit, they are Christians.

But is this really Christianity?

While it doesn't give God pleasure that any should perish, if no one fulfills His standard, would it cost Him anything to say as He said before: "I will destroy man whom I have created from the face of the earth; both man, and beast, and the creeping thing, and the fowls of the air; for it repents me that I have made them." (Gen 6:7).

"GOD saw that the wickedness of man *was* great in the earth, and *that* every intent of the thoughts of his heart *was* only evil continually And the Lord was sorry that he had made man on the earth, and he was grieved him in his heart." (Gen 6:5-6).

Nothing has changed about man and nothing has changed about God. He is still the twice Holy God; the same yesterday, today and forever.

There is a substance God is looking for in man to get to Him and He will not lower His standard if He doesn't find it in anyone, people, group or culture, even the whole world.

When His Son hung on the tree with the sins of the world on His neck, God took His eyes away from Him. Jesus cried: "Eli, Eli lama sabachthani?" That is, "My God, My God, why have You forsaken Me?" (Mat 27:46).

God is of purer eyes to behold iniquity, regardless of whom it is found. That was why He sent Lucifer, the son of the morning out of heaven. He is still the same God.

God's standard is perfection. But we say "Only God can be perfect...We are just to do our best." That is a cunningly devised religious consolation to pacify sinning saints and saintly sinners. The problem is that 'we do our best,' when Christ has done everything. We are trying to find a way, when He has made the way.

Is our best good enough for God and can it ever be?

Our works, labor and effort may be good and commendable, but are nothing but filthy rags to God. Yet, there is an innate nature in man to give God service or worship. But we posses nothing to give to God. The only thing to do is to love Him. Everything we give to Him is like the offering of Cain. Good, but not godly. He will not accept it if it doesn't possess the only thing He is looking for – love.

Jesus emphasized that love is the greatest commandment: to love the Lord your God with all your heart.

Despite the towering commendations for the church of Ephesus, Jesus told them: "...Nevertheless I have this against you, that you have left your first love." (Rev 2:2-4).

Jesus is the first love of the Father to us. His verdict is our only guarantee and admission ticket to heaven. He is the mediator between God and man. He is the love of God to the world now, but soon, He will be the judgment of God to the world.

God will be looking for Jesus in us, not works in us.
We must be like Jesus, just like He was like us while on earth. We must be conformed to His image and likeness.

He must be formed is us. We must grow and mature to the full stature of Christ.

Paul said even if he gave his body to be burned, gave all he had to the poor and so on, without love, he was nothing. So are we.

At the marriage feast of the Lamb with God in heaven in honor of His Son, Jesus, God waits on His Son to make the final verdict on everyone that claims to know Him. Our great and commendable works will not be a consideration.

While many would say to Him: "Lord, Lord, have we not prophesied in thy name? And in thy name have cast out devils? And in thy name done many wonderful works? And then will I profess unto them, I never knew you: depart from me, ye that work iniquity!" (Mat 7:22-23KJV).

How could people do such wonderful works, but to Jesus, they are all works of iniquity? Our wonderful works, without God's first love is iniquity to God. He did not deny the wonderful works, but those are not the qualification to heaven. He knows their works, but does not know them.

Christ must KNOW us, just like Adam 'knew his wife and she conceived." Only when Christ knows us in the sense of intimacy through relationship with Him can we bear fruits for Him.

As His bride, the groom must KNOW us. That is the only verdict that will open the gates of heaven to us. Would Christ, the Groom say to you, His bride: "I know you" or He would say, "I know you not...?"

You have been invited to the feast. But the King still requires you to be in your wedding garment. Christ is our garment. We must be clothed in His righteousness. So that when Father God looks at us, He would see Christ in us, not works.

My prayer is that this book will awaken believers to this salient revelation. It does God or us no good if our works are acceptable to Him, but we are not. He wants us, not our works.

1
IMAGE AND LIKENESS

"Beloved, now are we the children of God; and it has not been revealed what we shall be, but we know that when He is revealed, we shall be like Him, for we shall see Him as He is." (1Joh 3:2)

The Commendation

JESUS wrote letters to the seven Churches of Asia through John in the book of Revelation. Among them was the Church at Ephesus. She was one of the most active assemblies at that time. Jesus commended their works and efforts saying:

"I know your works, your labor, your patience, and that you cannot bear those who are evil. And you have tested those who say they are apostles and are not, and have found them liars; and you have persevered and

1

have patience, and have labored for My name's sake and have not become weary... But this you have, that you hate the deeds of the Nicolaitans, which I also hate." (Rev 2:3,6).

These are towering credentials only few churches, past or present can perhaps measure up to. However, despite Jesus' commendations to this Church, He shocked them by saying:

"Nevertheless I have this against you, that you have left your first love." (Rev 2:4).

He unquestionably found commendable works in the assembly, but that was not what He was looking for. He was looking for the requirement to get to God; their first love. It turned out to be the only thing He did not find in them. The first love is Jesus Himself, He is the first love of the Father to us (Joh 3:16).

In many believers' lives or assemblies today, there may be similar or even greater works, labor and other wonderful efforts. Many of these may be as commendable as, if not more than, that of the Church at Ephesus, but in Jesus' assessment, the love of Him is the foundation, and it is superior to all other things. It is the only requirement to God. Jesus is the way, the truth and the life. He said:

"...No one comes to the Father except through Me." *(John 14:6)* .

Revealed in Us

When the world was on the verge of destruction, God loved the world so much, and Christ is the evidence of that love. He is the manifest image and likeness of God on earth (Heb 1:3) to redeem man. The same likeness must be revealed in us. The world must see it in us, God must see it, too, before we can get back to Him.

The only thing that made Nebuchadnezzar, king of Babylon to bow to and believe the Lord God was the image and likeness of the Son of God he saw with Shadrach, Meshach and Abednego in the furnace of fire he threw them into for refusing to bow and worship his own image. To the three Hebrew men, their first love was God, and they displayed and maintained the love, even in the face of death. (Dan 3).

People must see the likeness of the Son of God in us, even in our darkest moment (2Cor 1:9). That must be our testimony. That was the testimony of the early believers which made the world to call them Christians, i.e., little Christs (Acts 11:26). We must be known by our resemblance of Him, not only by our confession.

If God created us in His image and likeness,

He will look for the same in us when we meet with Him. He will not look for our works.

Jesus did not find His image in the people and the Church at Ephesus. Will He find it in us and in our assembly, or will He find only good programs and activities?

The Only Requirement

God could have sent different species of creation to achieve His purpose on earth, other than man. He could have sent angels. But He chose to send man, created in His own very image and likeness. He could also have sent Jesus in a glorious body to the world to redeem humanity. The world would probably have believed Him (Luke 16:27-31).

But, although He was God in heaven, He came to the earth in the likeness of man *"and dwelt among us, and we beheld His glory, the glory as of the only begotten of the Father, full of grace and truth." (John 1:14).*

That was necessary to redeem man (Rom 8:3). To come to the earth, you must be man-like, to get to heaven, you must be God-like. So, Jesus was the perfect God-man. As God in the image of man, and as man in the image of God.

'*Therefore, in all things He had to be made like His*

brethren, that He might be a merciful and faithful High Priest in things pertaining to God, to make propitiation for the sins of the people." (Heb 2:17).

We also as man, must be in the image of God, for that is how we were created and that is how we must return to God.

The two times God sent man to earth, He made them come in His image (Adam and Jesus). If His image is not found in anyone, he cannot return to God.

Only the love of God, Jesus, (our first love) can make us to conform to that image. That is our only passport to God.

Before Saul met with the Lord, he said:

'*I advanced in Judaism beyond many of my contemporaries in my own nation, being more exceedingly zealous for the traditions of my fathers.*"

But when he met the Lord and was called into the ministry, he said:

"*It pleased God, who separated me from my mother's womb and called me through His grace, to reveal His Son in me, that I might preach Him among the Gentiles, I did not immediately confer with flesh and blood,*" (Gal 1:15-16. Emphasis mine).

God had to reveal His Son in Paul (Christ's image), in order to be able to preach among the heathens, otherwise, his preaching would have been in vain. John said:

'Beloved, now we are children of God; and it has not yet been revealed what we shall be, but we know that when He is revealed, we shall be like Him, for we shall see Him as He is." (1Joh 3:2).

God did not create us to be what we want to be or do what we want to do. He saves us that we may come to Him and take on His image and likeness. He saves us to do His will, not ours (Eph 1:4-5).

Paul said to the Churches at Corinth and Galatia respectively:

'For I determined not to know anything among you except Jesus Christ and Him crucified. (1Cor 2:2).

'My little children, for whom I labor in birth again until Christ is formed in you." (Gal 4:19).

Our 'travail' (labor, works or efforts) must be that Christ be formed in us and we are conformed to His image and likeness (Rom 8:29). As much as Christ is the express image and glory of God, we must be the image and glory of Christ (Heb. 1:3; John 17; 11,22). He must be formed in us and in our gatherings.

God gave us His Son and He is looking for only what He gave to us, not what we can give to Him.

Not finding His own image and likeness in the church at Ephesus, Jesus warned them to

6

repent or He would remove their lampstand (Holy Spirit).

> '*Remember therefore from where you have fallen; repent and do the first works, or else I will come to you quickly and remove your lampstand from its place—unless you repent.* (Rev 2:5).

Old Glory

The church at Ephesus had 'fallen', yet was still active in commendable works. This shows clearly what wonderful works fallen man (or assembly) can do for God: grow church, perform miracles, save souls, be involved in missions, yet fallen! This is so because, '*For the gifts and the calling of God are irrevocable.* (Rom 11:29).

The riches of the glory of God is when Christ is in us daily. The grace of yesterday is not sufficient for the task of today. His steadfast love is new every morning (Lam 3:23).

Christ, not works is the hope of our glory (Col 1:27). He does this by changing '*our lowly body that it may be conformed to His glorious body, according to the working by which He is able even to subdue all things to Himself.*" (Php 3:21).

He alone can work this out in our lives on a continuous basis. Only when we are in Him can

He do that. We will then be conformed to Him and not to the world, and we will be transformed by the renewing of our mind. Then, also, we will be able to *"prove what is that good and acceptable and perfect will of God."* (Rom 12:2).

Union with Him

Eve was taken out of Adam when he was at rest in God. God caused a deep sleep to fall on Him, and only then could He bring out the bone of his bone and the flesh of his flesh. (Gen 2:21-23). Eve was in Adam when he was created. We are in Christ as the bone of His bone and the flesh of His flesh. To be taken out of Christ as Eve was taken out of Adam, we must be at rest in Christ, not busy running around for Him.

Only He can cause a deep sleep to fall on us and only then can He work on us as He worked on Adam, removing his rib to make a help meet for him (Gen 2:2). As Eve was presented to Adam, Christ must present us to the Father as a

'glorious church, not having spot or wrinkle or any such thing, but that she should be holy and without blemish." (Eph 5:27).

Through union with his bride, Eve, Adam *'begot a son in his own likeness, after his image, and named him Seth."* (Gen 5:3). Through union

8

with Christ in the Spirit, we must be made to be in the full image and likeness of Christ. This is when we become the true sons and daughters of our Father.

'Beloved, now we are children of God; and it has not yet been revealed what we shall be, but we know that when He is revealed, we shall be like Him, for we shall see Him as He is." (1John 3:2).

2
KNOWING HIM

"Now Adam knew Eve his wife, and she conceived and bore Cain, and said, "I have acquired a man from the LORD." (Gen 4:1).

Relationship

WE cannot be formed into the image and likeness of someone we never knew or met. Yet, that is just the beginning; we must grow in Him and mature unto a perfect man, unto the measure of the stature of the FULLNESS of Christ (Eph 4:13), not just a part. This can only happen when there is relationship.

Good works, effort or labor cannot replace relationship, even in the natural family. They may be wonderful but cannot produce seed or life.

How wonderful can a partner be who showers his / her spouse with all good things and words but denies him / her of the ultimate intimate expression of relationship? Can couples be so busy that they cannot give themselves to each other? Or can things, sweet words or noble activities replace intimacy?

Christ wants intimate relationship with us more than our greatest labor for Him. Only then can He be formed in us.

Fruitfulness

A good tree is not just a big, tall, green and flowery one, with branches, shades, leaves, but no fruit. Jesus cursed the tree that did not produce fruit to satisfy His hunger (Mar 11:14). He said to his disciples:

"Every branch in Me that does not bear fruit He takes away, and every branch that bears fruit He prunes, that it may bear more fruit… Abide in Me, and I in you. As the branch cannot bear fruit of itself, unless it abides in the vine, neither can you, unless you abide in Me. I am the vine, you are the branches. He who abides in Me, and I in him, bears much fruit; for without Me ye can do nothing. If anyone does not abide in Me, he is cast out as a branch and is withered; and they gather them and throw them into

the fire, and they are burned." (John 15:2,4-6).

Fruitfulness in a relationship comes only by 'knowing' one another (intimacy). Like Adam 'knew' his wife, Christ must 'know' us, only then are we enabled by Him (through the deposit of His grace in us) to bear fruit for Him.

"Adam knew his wife, and she conceived..." (Gen 4:1).

When the husband knows his wife, seed is raised in his name. When Christ knows us, He will form Himself in us.

Denial

Jesus denies some people entry to heaven because He does not 'know' them. He said to them, *"I know you not".* But they claimed that they had done many wonderful things for God, including prophesying, healing in His name, doing many wonderful things, working and laboring for God.

When the disciples asked questions on this, He said to them:

"Strive to enter through the narrow gate, for many, I say to you, will seek to enter and will not be able." (Luke 13:23-24).

Seeking means a spirited and deliberate

EFFORT. Why would people truly SEEK to enter, but will not be able to? Because entry is only by knowing. It is the only way we can look like Him. It is not activities, but relationship.

In this parable, the master of the house (Jesus) shut the door, and the people *"begin to stand outside and knock at the door, saying, "Lord, Lord, open for us," and He will answer and say to you, "I do not know you, where you are from."* (Luke 13:25).

The interesting thing in this parable is that the people stood up to knock at the Master's door, called Him Lord and demanded that He open to them on the basis of their works for Him. This means, it is possible to stand for Jesus, knock at the heaven's gate through prayer and acknowledge Him as Lord and yet we be none of His.

The people argued further:

"We ate and drank IN YOUR PRESENCE, and You taught in our streets..." (Luke 13:26. Emphasis mine).

Notice the wonderful works they did for Him. They ate and drank IN HIS PRESENCE (a form of observance of ordinances, like the Lord's Table, baptism, prophecy, etc), and also listened to His words (bible study, sermons, seminars, etc). No one could truly square up to his master with these claims if he really didn't do them. But Jesus tells them emphatically:

*"I tell you, I do not **know** you, where ye are from. Depart from Me, all you workers of iniquity."* (Vs 27).

Jesus did not deny them entry on the basis of their claims, but because He did not know them; He was not formed in them, therefore, He did not see Himself in them, though He saw wonderful works.

There is a marked difference between knowing the Lord and working for the Lord. We cannot get to God on the basis of the latter (Eph 2:9; Rom 4:2; Rom 9:11; 2Tim 1:9). Relationship makes us to abide in Him and bear fruit for Him (John 15:4,6,7).

To Know Him

Our greatest labor in people's lives should be that Christ be formed in them, not making them Christians, our disciples or followers, or to meet their needs. Paul said to the Corinthian church in 2Cor 11:2:

"… I have betrothed you to one husband, that I may present you as a chaste virgin to Christ."

While Jesus prepared for His final departure, He prayed what could be called the 'Lord's Prayer' for the disciples.

"As You have given him authority over all flesh, that He should give eternal life to as many as You have given Him. And this is life eternal, that THEY MAY KNOW YOU, the only true God, and Jesus Christ, whom You have sent." (John 17:2-3. Emphasis mine). Here we see the definition of eternal life: that we may know Christ.

Towards the end of Apostle Paul's life, he also prayed a passionate prayer:

"That I MAY KNOW HIM and the power of His resurrection, and the fellowship of His sufferings, being ***conformed*** *to his death."* (Php 3:10. Emphasis mine).

How embarrassing can Paul's statement be in the above passage! Despite all his labor for several decades, at the end of his life, his prayer was that he might **know** Christ.

Paul knew that knowing Christ is the only key to getting to heaven, not his missionary trips, his labor or activities. This should be our most important duty, too, more than ministry activities.

However, knowing Him is one thing, Him knowing us is another. The latter is what counts in heaven.

In Acts 19, we read the account of the seven sons of Sceva. They were having a sort of deliverance on some who were possessed with demons in "the name of the Lord Jesus thus:

"We exorcise you by the Jesus whom Paul preaches…" (Acts 19:13).

But the evil spirit asked them a very salient question:

"Jesus I know, and Paul I know; but who are you?" Not being able to provide a satisfactory answer, *"the evil spirit was leaped on them, overpowered them, and prevailed against them, so that they fled out of that house naked and wounded."* (Acts 19:16).

The evil spirit fractured their claim of knowing Jesus and His power. Even though they demonstrated knowing Jesus by attempting to carry out deliverance in His name, it was clear that Jesus did not know them.

The same evil spirits once said to Jesus:

"Let us alone! What have we to do with You, Jesus of Nazareth? Did you come to destroy us? I know who You are-the Holy One of God. (Mark 1:24, Mark 5:7; Luke 8:28).

If You Do Well

Consistently throughout the scriptures, when people's offering were not received, or their claim of knowing God or Christ was denied, it

17

was followed by a revolt or rebellion.

When Cain's offering was rejected by God, he *"was very angry, and his countenance fell."* (Gen 4:5). He did not receive the message. God did not have 'respect' for his offering, not because it was bad, but because it was not what God required.

Cain must have taken a second look at his offering and wondered why it was rejected by God when it was the fruit of his labor. But God asked him:

"Why are you angry? And why has your countenance fallen? If you do well, will you not be accepted? and if you do not do well, sin lies at the door. And its desire is for you but you should rule over it." (Gen 4:6-7).

This is the key: 'if you do well, you will be accepted'. He did not 'do well'; he did not give God what God required, but rather, he gave his own effort, labor and work, albeit, the best. God is not looking for our best, but what He requires.

It is always crushing when our best is not good enough. The rejection can lead to rebellion and backsliding. But God has always made His mind known. There is no sacrifice without the blood, not just any blood, but such as is pleasing to God, the one He chose; like Jesus.

"He has shown you, O man, what is good; And what

does the LORD require of You, but to do justly, To love mercy, And to walk humbly with your God?" (Mic 6:8).

Sin lies at the door of everyone who would not do what His Lord requires from him, but his own.

"And that servant, who knew his master's will, and did not prepare himself or do according to his will, shall be beaten with many stripes." (Luke12:47).
"...There will be weeping and gnashing of teeth." (Luke 13:28).

The church at Ephesus must have received Jesus' message with surprise and marvel, despite all their works, labor and efforts. 'How could that be' they must have wondered!

Our claim could also be that we not only know Him, but we love and adore Him with all our hearts. But what if Christ says He does not know us? What surprise will break over our faces?

The surprise could lead to rebellion in our hearts and total backsliding, if not received with humility. If we resist God's verdict, sin lies at our door. Cain killed his brother, Abel. We can also rebel. We must not allow offence in our hearts. Jesus told the church at Ephesus to repent.

The foolish virgins could accuse the wise of not helping them. The people shut out of heaven could also accused the Master of insensitivity and ingratitude, despite all their labor and sacrifice for the Lord. Martha took offence in Jesus and asked if He didn't care. (Luke 10:40). But Jesus' response to Martha was firm. It was similar to God's response to Cain:

(*"If you do well, would you not be accepted?"*) Jesus said to her: *"Mary has chosen that good part, which will not be taken away from her."* (Luke 10:42).

If we do well, we will be accepted. But if we do not, then sin lies at the door. Only one thing is needed: knowing Him and Him knowing us. This can happen when we present our selves, not our works, to Him as a living sacrifice. That is our reasonable service (Rom 12:1).

3
WHAT TO DO.

"... For without Me you can do nothing." (Joh 15:5)

No Other Foundation

WHY do men think there is something to do on their own to get to God? If there was anything to do to get to God, then, Jesus needn't have come! The only thing to do is to know what God has done (the way He has provided) for man to get to Him, and that is Jesus.

Religion is not the way to God. Christianity, ministry, charity or activities are not; Jesus is. He said:

"I am the way, the truth, and the life. No one comes to the Father except by Me." (John 14:6).

Jesus *"obtained a more excellent ministry... He is also the Mediator of a better covenant, which was established upon better promises. For if that first covenant had been faultless, then no place would have been sought for a second."* (Heb 8:6-7).

Among those who asked Jesus what to do to have eternal life was the rich young ruler. He wanted to know WHAT ELSE to do, because he had done all 'from his youth'. Jesus told him just what to do: *"Go, sell what you have and give to the poor..."* (Mat 19:21; Mark 10:21).

Our works and efforts must come to the place of ruin if we must gain Christ. Paul said:

"But what things were gain to me, these I counted loss for Christ. Yet indeed I count all things loss for the excellence of the knowledge of Christ Jesus my Lord, for whom I have suffered the loss of all things, and count them as rubbish, that I may gain Christ." (Php 3:7-8).

Coming to Christ is like a drowning man that needs a rescuer. The only thing he needs do is to trust the rescuer and yield himself entirely to him without struggle. *"By strength shall no man prevail"* (1Sam 2:9). The only way that leads to God is the way of the cross and we must come just as we are, as naked as a newborn baby.

Empty*ing* Vessels

After Jesus told the young ruler what to do to make heaven on his own merit, (to sell all he had), He then told him God's requirement: *"Come, follow me."* (Mat 19:21). That is the only [simple] thing to do to get to heaven, but he must first empty himself of his achievements (naked as new born baby) and give the proceeds to the poor (not even to Jesus) before he could follow Him.

We must willingly lay down our achievements and abilities before the Lord in exchange for His grace. Grace is divine ability to do God's will. It has to be what He does, not what we do. He does all His works by Himself, using willing hands, empty*ing* vessels.

We may have great burdens for the lost, God does also. He said: *"The harvest truly is great, but the laborers are few."* (Luke 10:2). He has also made a way to save them. His way has nothing to do with the best of our ideas. We may have burden in our hearts seeing the enormous need of the Savior around us, and that may create a desire in our hearts to labor to save the world. But we cannot. We can only do as much as what He has asked us to do, nothing more. He told us what to do:

"*Pray the Lord of the harvest, that he would send forth laborers into his harvest.*" (Luke 10:2).

We can only preach to the world, we cannot save the world, only He can, when we pray. God does nothing, except in answer to prayers.

If You Love Me...

If our love for Jesus does not culminate in obeying Him, it is not a genuine love. He said to the disciples:

"*If ye love me, keep my commandments.*" (John 14:15).

"*And Samuel said, Has the LORD as great delight in burnt offerings and sacrifices. As in obeying the voice of the LORD? Behold, to obey is better than sacrifice, And to heed than the fat of rams.*" (1Sam 15:22).

He can save the lost, only if we obey. He said:

"*If My people, who are called by my name will humble themselves, and pray and seek my face, and turn from their wicked ways, then I will hear from heaven, and will forgive their sin and will heal their land.* (2Chr 7:14). Only if His people will obey!

Why do we seem to cry more than the

bereaved in our efforts and activities for the lost? If we obey Him, souls will be saved and it is He that will save them, not us, not our works or efforts. He came for them (Luke 19:10). We cannot love them more than He. He left His glory in heaven, endured the shame, and died on the cross to bring them to God. The best we can do is to do exactly what He asks us to do, not to run ahead of Him to fix things for Him.

Our line-up of activities, programs, missionary journeys, etc, must be in obedience to his commands. He is waiting on us to do our part, which is to pray. He said:

"And I, if I am lifted up from the earth, will draw all peoples unto Myself." (John 12:32).

If we love Him, we will lift Him up more than lift up the banner of our ministry, church, organization or activities.

Service Without His Will

All our achievements, abilities and zeal can be a great burden and hindrance to God's plans and operations, rather than the help we intend it to be. This can happen if we run ahead of Him to offer Him sacrifice rather than the obedience He requires.

Saul was a victim of this. He labored to give God service without His will. His service was a persecution of God, but unknown to him. (Acts 9:4) He later wrote to Timothy and said:

"I thank Christ Jesus our Lord who has enabled me, because He counted me faithful, putting me into the ministry, although I was formerly a blasphemer, a persecutor, and an insolent man; but I obtained mercy, because I did it ignorantly in unbelief." (1Tim 1:12-13).

We fall into this category many times in our gatherings and fellowships. Our worship, most of the times, is always in culture and in traditions rather than in spirit and in truth. We give God our own best, but not what He desires.

God appreciates our best: special programs to bring numerical growth to our assembly, or revival to win souls to the kingdom and other mission activities, educational endeavors and other charitable works. They are commendable, but Jesus is not coming for them. He is coming for individuals within whom He is formed and matured in. He is coming for His bride of whom He is the head.

Jesus wants us, not our works. He said: *"Come to Me..."* (Matt 11:28). He did not ask us to bring the best works to Him. He wants relationship with us, not activities from us.

We must decrease, that He may increase (John 3:30). We must come to the end of self when there is nothing else to flaunt. No beautiful church building to point to, no great organizational structure to cherish or decorated altar to deify. Also, no camp-site to consecrate, all mission activities to the poor, growing membership, anniversaries, crusades, conferences, network of parishes, etc, no longer matter. These are good, but only to have treasures in heaven, but not necessary to make heaven. We can only make heaven with Christ.

4

THE LEAVEN

"Your glorying is not good. Do you not know that a little leaven leavens the whole lump?" (1 Cor 5:6)

Just Obey

God's definition of sin is not in the quantity, or degree, but in the presence, even in the smallest particle.

One sin is enough to make one a sinner, and no sinner gets to God without repentance. It all starts very small and matures. It takes a little stain to spoil the wedding garment: all unrighteousness is sin (1John 5:17). Sin is missing the mark, regardless of the degree.

Like the Law in the Old Testament, if anyone

fulfils all the laws, but fails in one, he is guilty of all (Jas 2:10). This is the same in God's operation of salvation. Simple obedience supersedes great labor. Grace through faith is the qualification, not work through labor.

The quantity of our labor is nothing compared to the smallest of our obedience. Faith in what God can do if we obey Him must be our greatest work, labor and effort. Faith like the mustard seed Jesus said:

"If you can believe, all things are possible to him who believes." (Mar k9:23).

We must labor to press in to enter into that glorious rest when we give Him the chance to do what He alone can do through us to the world. Obedience is the key.

As good as these are, it's a snare to the end time church. It disrupts the eternal plan of God: that Christ be formed in us.

Jesus asked Peter:

"Do you love Me more than this, then feed My sheep." (John 21:16).

To feed the sheep doesn't look like a lot of works.

When God put Adam in the Garden of Eden, He simply asked him to *"dress it and to keep it"*.

How difficult was that? God had already planted the Garden, He only needed them to tend it.

"... And out of the ground made the LORD God made every tree grow that is pleasant to the sight and good for food... a river went out of Eden to water the garden, and from thence it was parted and became four riverheads." (Gen 2:9-10).

God already did the major work; all Adam needed to do was to freely eat from every tree of the Garden but one. God also sent mist from the earth, and watered the whole face of the ground. He also asked Adam to give names to all the animals at his convenience, and whatever name he called each one, that was its name.

Upon all that, God asked him to *"be fruitful, and multiply; fill the earth and subdue it; have dominion over the fish of the sea, over the birds of the air, and over every living thing that move on the earth."* (Gen 1:28). What a wonderful God!

As if all this was not enough, *"The LORD God said, 'it is not good that the man should be alone; I will make him a helper comparable to him."* (Gen 2:18).

All Adam needed to do was to fulfill the greatest command; to love God enough to obey Him. But Adam was busy with a little experiment with sin and was guilty of the first love. We can be busy working for God and be guilty loving God. What man can do for God (and we can do a lot) is not the same as what God requires us to do for Him (1Sam 15:22). The former is religion, and Satan is the author of religion (2Cor 11:14).

Jesus said the greatest commandment is to *"love the Lord your God with all your mind. This is the first and great commandment."* (Mat 22:37-38).

Religion

Our strength is in our obedience (faith), not our actions or works (religion). In works, there is man's boasting…

"In your name we have healed the sick…"

"… in your name we have done many wonderful works…" (Mat 7:22).

But it is *"not of works, lest anyone should boast."* (Eph 2:9). Religion has its own reward (1Cor 3:8), but faith is the basis of salvation (Rom 5:1; 2Tim 3:15). It is faith that saves and without faith we cannot please God (Heb 11:6).

Works is religion. It has its own reward, but independent of salvation. You don't have to be saved to have good works, but you have to be saved to get a reward for your good works. You don't have to be a Christian or believe in Jesus

Christ to engage in good works. There are probably various religious organizations with wonderful and charitable works affecting millions of lives positively around the world.

"Pure and undefiled before God and the Father is this: to visit orphans and widows in their trouble, and to keep oneself unspotted from the world." (Jas 1:27).

Would they be rewarded for their works? Yes, abundantly too, if they make heaven.

At the judgment, two books would be opened, first the book of life, which is for admission to heaven; second, the book of rewards in which every man is judged according to their works. John said:

"And I saw the dead, small and great, standing before God, and the books were opened. And another book was opened, which is the Book of Life. And the dead were judged according to their works, by the things which were written in the books… And anyone was not found written in the Book of Life was cast into the lake of fire." (Rev 20:12-15).

So, work is not the basis for making heaven, it is faith. Faith and religion are direct opposite of one another. Religion is good for reward; however, faith is the 'entry level' to Christian life. It goes on to having relationship with Christ and culminates at 'knowing Him'. Knowing Him is becoming like Him, being formed into His image and likeness. This enables us to bear fruit for Him on earth and to hear "Well done, good and faithful servant" in heaven.

Salvation comes first, without which there will be no reward even for the greatest works.

Jesus warned the disciples to *"take heed and beware of the leaven of the Pharisees and of the Sadducees."* (Mat 16:6) - Doctrine of works.

Zeal

The enthusiasm of taking works to a fanatical level is called zeal. Zeal for religious works and activities destroys. Paul was there before he came to Christ. He was active in works for God and persecuted the church of God, even *"to death, binding and delivering into prisons both men and women."* (Acts 22:4).

He said further:

"I punished them often in every synagogue, and compelled them to blaspheme; and being exceedingly enraged against them, I persecuted them even to foreign cities... that beyond measure I persecuted the church of God beyond measure and tried to destroy it." (Acts 26:11; 1Cor 15:9; Gal 1:13).

In his letter to the Philippian Church:
"Concerning zeal, persecuting the church; concerning

the righteousness which is in the law, blameless." (Php 3:6).

He however thought that he was doing God a service. When he came to faith, he confessed that he *"was formerly a blasphemer, and an insolent man; but I obtained mercy because I did it ignorantly in unbelief."* (1Tim 1:13).

David said:

*"Zeal for your house has eaten me up, And the reproaches of those who reproached You have fallen on me." (*Psa 69:9).

That is dangerous without proper knowledge of God's eternal plans. That was the little leaven for Israel, Paul said of Israel: *"I bear them witness that they have a zeal for God, but not according to knowledge."* (Rom 10:2).

Zeal for God's works, without the knowledge of what God really requires can become sheer fanatism. It happened to Israel, the Pharisees, the church at Ephesus and indeed the last day church and religious people in the world. Jesus warned his disciples to *"beware ye of the leaven of the Pharisees, which is hypocrisy."* (Luke 12:1).

It is leaving what is to be done undone and doing so well what should not be done at all.

Zeal subjects men to ordinances of

performance of things which has a show of wisdom, worship and service. Beware of the Pharisee teachings, which replaces faith in God with religion. The Pharisees, the Sadducees and the Scribes liked to *"go about in long robes, love greetings in the marketplaces, the best seats in the synagogues, and the best places at feasts"* (Luke 20:46).

Paul called the Pharisees and Sadducees *"dogs"* and *"evil workers."* He went further to say that:

> *"We are the circumcision, who worship God in the Spirit, rejoice in Christ Jesus, and have no confidence in the flesh."* (Php 3:2-3). Paul warned further: *"Beware lest any man cheat you through philosophy and empty deceit, according to the tradition of men, according to the basic principles of the world, and not according to Christ."* (Col 2:8).

5
FIRST LOVE

"And now abide faith, hope, love, these three; but the greatest of these is love." (1Cor 13:13)

The Love Test

THE mention of the word 'first love' may provoke an examination of our hearts to know if we truly love Jesus or not. Our love might be just a statement and not a reality. But right now, we would say it is real and that is straight from our hearts. Our worship, tithe, membership, commitment and other activities are evidences.

But just like *"each one's work will become clear; for the Day will declare it, because it will be revealed by fire; and the fire will test each one's work, of what sort it is."* (1Cor 3:13). So also our love.

When Peter's claim of love for Christ was put to the test, it had no standing. He had earlier said to Jesus:

"I will never leave you, even though all the rest do!" (Mat 26:33GNB).

But when the trial came, it was soon revealed that he loved his life more than his Lord; he denied his Lord three times before he realized it, although not willingly.

"Now Peter sat outside in the courtyard. And a servant girl came to him saying, "You also were with Jesus or Galilee. But he denied it before them all, saying "I do not know what you are saying. And when he had gone out to the gateway, another girl saw him and said to those who were there, "This fellow also was with Jesus of Nazareth. But again he denied with an oath, " do not know the Man!" and a little later those who stood by came and said to Peter, "Surely you also are one of them, for your speech betrays you. Then he began to curse and swear, saying, "I do not know the Man! Immediately a rooster crowed." (Mat 26:69-74)

Many times, *"the spirit indeed is willing, but the flesh is weak."* (Mat 26:41).

Judas' love for Jesus was evidenced by his betrayal (Mat 26:49). He might have thought that

Jesus was such a superman and would spring surprises and escape from their midst as He had done several times in the past (John 8:59; John 10:39). So, betraying Him would be smart, as Jesus would not be arrested and He could keep the money having done his part. His love was money, not his Lord (John 12:6). He loved position too.

When Jesus announced to His disciples that His kingdom was not of this world, and that He would not fight Caesar, many of His disciples who had thought they would hold important positions when Jesus became the king of Israel were disappointed. Judas was perhaps more disappointed. He must have decided there and then to help himself out in order to achieve his love [of money and position]. He went to the chief priests and said to them:

"What are you willing to give me if I deliver Him to you? And they counted out to him thirty pieces of silver. So from that time he sought opportunity to betray Him." (Mat 26:15-16).

While Peter and Judas didn't particularly pass the love test for their Lord, it was evidenced that Peter later regarded not his life again, but preached Christ boldly, even when it was a suicide to do so (Acts 2:14-37).

All the disciples had time to prove their love

for their Lord by laying down their lives for Him. If He died for us and His Spirit is in us, we will love Him up to the point of laying down our lives for Him, unless we are bastards.

Jesus said:

"He who loves father or mother more than Me is not worthy of me. And he who loves son or daughter more than Me is not worthy of Me. And he does not take his cross and follow after Me, is not worthy of Me. He who finds his life shall lose it, and he who loses his life for My sake will find it." (Mat 10:37-39).

A man came from Judea to Caesarea, to the house of Philip the Evangelist. He was named Agabus. He was a prophet.

"He took Paul's belt, bound his own hands and feet, and said, "Thus says the Holy Spirit, 'So shall the Jews at Jerusalem bind the man who owns this belt, and deliver him into the hands of the Gentiles'". Now when we heard these things, both we and those from that place pleaded with him not to go up to Jerusalem. Then Paul answered, "What do you mean by weeping and breaking my heart? For I am ready not only to be bound, but also to die at Jerusalem for the name of the Lord Jesus." (Acts 21:11-13).

If we are not ready to die for what we believe in, then, it is not worth living for. Our testimony is not only to live for Jesus, but also to die for Him.

"For we know that if our earthly house of this tent, is destroyed, we have a building from God, a house not made with hands, eternal in the heavens." (2Cor 5:1).

Stephen's recognition came through his faith, not his works. His first testimony in the church was that he was a man *"full of faith and of the Holy Spirit"* (Acts 6:5). This relationship later made him *"full of faith and power, did great wonders and signs among the people."* (Acts 6:8). When we love Him, He will release to us the treasures of His kingdom to function; that we may love Him more.

Stephen became a threat to the government. They disputed with him as regards the matter of his faith and love for his Lord and Master, but they *"were not able to resist the wisdom and the Spirit by which he spoke. Then they secretly induced men to say "We have heard him speak blasphemous words against Moses, and God." And they stirred up the people, the elders, and the scribes; and they came upon him, seized him, and brought him to the council. They also set up false witnesses who said, "This man does cease to speak blasphemous words against this holy place, and the law; for we have heard him say, that this Jesus of Nazareth shall destroy this place and change the customs which*

Moses delivered us. " (Acts 6:11-14).

In all these allegations, Stephen was unruffled. When they looked at him, *"all who sat in the council, looking steadfastly at him, saw his face as the face of an angel"* (Acts 6:15). Yet they stoned him to death. He did not deny his Lord and Master. He loved Him to death.

Sometimes we ask ourselves if we believed the same Jesus and if we are going to the same heaven as these men of great faith in God, who loved their Lord to the point of death. All that the last days church is left with in terms of Christianity is work, activities, programs and denominations. Jesus asked that if He came back, would He find faith on earth? – the old time faith, not the new style religion of rascality.

Works of Iniquity

The church at Ephesus had great works: they could not even stand those who were evil; they tried those who said they were apostles, and found them to be liars. They had patience, labor, and did not give up. They even hated the deeds of the Nicolaitans, which Christ also hates. (Rev 2:2,3,6) Yet, Jesus didn't find Himself (first love) in them.

In Matthew 7:22, Jesus Himself said:

"Many will say to me in that day, Lord, Lord, have we not prophesied in Your name? cast out demons in Your name, and done many wonders in Your name?" (Mat 7:22).

Yet, Jesus called them, "workers of iniquity". He said to them that He did not know them.

In our hearts, iniquity may denote sin. But in this context, it does not. Sinners may not stand before God to claim any righteous deeds, but these people did. Note that Jesus called them 'workers of iniquity', not 'workers of sin'.

Iniquity, in this context is synonymous to bringing great works first, and Christ following. Jesus rebuked the Pharisees for doing what was necessary but neglecting what was greater (Luke 11:42).

Our works for Christ must not overshadow our love for Him. Love brings relationship, even with Jesus. But mere work without a relationship with Him is wickedness and iniquity to God, it is like the sacrifice of Cain. King Solomon said:

"The sacrifice of the wicked is abomination; How much more when he brings it with wicked intent?" (Pro 21:27).

Works is performance. *"Now to him who works, the wages are not counted as grace but as debt. But to him who does not work but believes on Him who justifies the ungodly, his faith is counted for righteousness."* (Rom 4:4-5).

God will not judge us on performance of work, but on acceptance of His love. Love is the greatest of all. Works is law, love is grace. By the works of the law shall no flesh be justified in His presence, but by grace we are saved (Gal 2:16; Eph 2:8).

We must be energized by the leading of God, not our burden for Him or the appeal of religion or denominational tradition. It is easy to replace relationship with Jesus with relationship with brethren. To Jesus, great and wonderful as this may be, it is iniquity.

Cold Love

Jesus said:

"Take heed that no one deceive you... because iniquity shall abound, the love of many shall wax cold." (Mat 24:3,12KJV).

This suggests that the 'many' once had the love, but it would gradually thaw out and turn cold because iniquity (works without relationship) shall 'abound', in the church.

Cain's offering was a demonstration of man's work for God without a relationship with Him, so also the church at Ephesus. The people whose master denied them entry in the parable and those denied entry by Jesus in heaven are further confirmation of this. Their works received commendations, but Jesus was looking for Himself first before He considers their good works. Without Himself, the good works automatically become filthy rags. It is better to eat a dry morsel with love than a sumptuous meal without it; it is wickedness.

The disciples understood the truth in Jesus statement:

"Enter by the narrow gate; for wide is the gate and broad is the way that leads to destruction, and there are many who go in by it. Because narrow is the gate ad difficult is the way which leads to life, and there are few who find it." (Mat 7:13-14). They saw it demonstrated in the encounter with the rich ruler, and that heaven is not by performance, but by obedience. They asked Him: *"Who then can be saved"*? (Luke 18:26).

In reply, Jesus emphasized the salient truth about love again:

"You shall love the Lord your God with all your heart, with all your soul, and with all your mind. This is the first and great commandment." (Mat 22:37-38; Mark 12:30).

To love the Lord God is the first and

greatest commandment, not to work for Him. Iniquity (i.e. busy working for God) turns the love of God in our hearts cold. Such work that makes our love for God to turn cold is the work of iniquity. It cannot be used as the passport to get to heaven. Love is the passport to heaven, first love, the love of Jesus in our hearts.

6
THE RESULT

"When the king came in to see the guests, he saw a man there who did not have a wedding garment. So He said to him, 'Friend, how did you come in here without a wedding garment?' And he was speechless..." (Mat 22:11-12).

No hiding place

Iniquity destroyed Satan's relationship with God in heaven. We know about this through the revelations God gave to prophet Ezekiel:

"You were in Eden, the garden of God; every precious stone was your covering; the sardius, topaz, and diamond, beryl, onyx, and jasper, sapphire, turquoise, and emerald with gold. The workmanship of your timbrels and pipes was prepared for you thee

on the day you were created. You were the anointed cherub who covers; I established you; you were on the holy mountain of God; you walked back and forth in the midst of the fiery stones. You were perfect in your ways from the day you were created, till iniquity was found in you." (Eze 28:13-15).

Everything seem to be going well for Lucifer *'till iniquity was found'* in him. The following verses reveal the progression of his many activities.

"By the abundance of your trading, you became filled with violence within and you sinned; therefore I cast you as profane thing out of the mountain of God; and I destroyed you, O covering cherub, from the midst of the fiery stones. Your heart was lifted up because of thy beauty; you corrupted your wisdom for the sake of your splendor. I cast you to the ground, I laid you before kings, that they might gaze at you." (Eze 28:16-17).

The Good News Bible Version puts it this way: *"You were busy buying and selling, and this led you to violence and sin."*

While the New King James Version calls his activities 'abundance of trading', the Good News Bible calls it 'busy buying and selling' through the 'abundance of traffic" which eventually filled his heart, instead of love, reverence and worship of God to fill his heart.

Just like many cannot manage success, many tend to lose their balance and forget God in times of abundance and or activities, not willingly. They remember Him again in times of adversity. Even if they do, God will not lower His standard for them. They will only find Him when they seek Him with all their hearts.

There is something in man that always looks for what to do and wants to be gratified. He wants a sense of performance, and a self satisfaction of physical involvement, not just an abstract worship in faith of an unseen Being. This makes people to mistake the physical expression of worship with worship itself, which is inner. This is how religion was birthed.

When we are busy 'buying and selling', i.e., involved in many activities, we tend to give little or no attention to the utmost responsibility. Care must be taken not to lose the major while pursuing the minor. We are saved to give Him glory, not to fulfill our own ambition or desire, no matter how godly. His Will is supreme and sovereign. We are created for His pleasure. Everything is from Him, in Him, of Him, by Him, through Him and to Him.

Often we hear the adage: "jack of all trade, master of none". This seemed to be the philosophy of Lucifer and he lost all. He lost the purpose of His creation. So did Adam and Eve. We can, too. There can be much movement truly, but no progress. We can be busy but guilty.

Adam and Eve were fulfilled with the communion they had with God in the cool of the day. God, too was. That is still God's original plan for us. But they desired more, perhaps, something more tangible and physical than just a spirit thing.

They entertained harmless fellowship with a stranger, a 'friend' beyond the Garden who introduced them to a new communion of activity rather than fellowship. God had said to them:

"Of every tree of the garden you may freely eat; but of the tree of the knowledge of good and evil you shall not eat, for in the day that you eat of it you shall surely die." (Gen 2:16-17). But the friend said, *"you will not surely die. For God knows that in the day you eat of it your eyes will be opened and you will be like God, knowing good and evil."* (Gen 3:4-5). They followed their friend's advice anyway.

The same desire has led to the introduction of many 'strange fires' in our meetings and gatherings in order to justify our sense of 'service' and worship. We want to have tangibility. But the truth is that *"God is Spirit, and those who worship Him must worship in Spirit and truth."* (John 4:24). We must come to Him by faith, not by works. We please Him by faith, not our works. We must believe that He is, and He is the rewarder of them who diligently seek Him.(Heb 11:6) That is the only way we can escape fighting with Satan in his own turf.

The Soul Realm

Jesus escaped through the word of God, not by proving to Satan through great works of turning stones to bread or jumping down from the pinnacle of the temple. (Mat 4:3-10). He could do it, but He did not. If he did, it is fighting Satan in his own turf. That alone is victory for him. He wants to make us work the work of God, rather than just loving Him.

The flesh will always desire to be gratified, but we must not fulfill the desire of the flesh by giving it want it wants like Eve did. (Rom 8:8; Gal 5:17, Gal 6:8).

Human expression through emotions, sentiments or other means do not bring us to God's presence, although it gives us a satisfaction. But God is not an emotional God. He watches over His words, not our emotions.

Shouting or dancing, for example maybe an outward expression of joy in the Holy Spirit in us, but the real joy is inner, not the shout or the dance.

Expression is not reality, but reality always comes with expression. Speaking in tongues does not mean the presence of the Holy Spirit, but when the Holy Spirit is present, tongues is an evidence (Acts 2:4; Acts 19:2-6; Acts 10:44-46).

We must not take hold of expressions such as dance or shout as the presence of the Holy Spirit. There can be much singing, dancing, shouting and other expression of joy but the Holy Spirit may not be present. But when the Holy Spirit is present, these expressions may be found. We must not, therefore institutionalize expressions. It is deceptive. It is religion. It is Satan.

Song is not worship, neither is lifting up hands or being quiet in His presence. These are outward expressions of worship, but the true worship is from our inside. These are soul manifestations, not spirit. We are spirit beings and God also is Spirit. We relate with God spirit to spirit, not soul to soul.

Paul encouraged us to speak to one another in Psalms, hymns and spiritual songs (Eph 5:20;

Col 3:16). But there are no spiritual songs. It is when spiritual people sing songs that makes the song spiritual. Otherwise, it can be sang by anyone anywhere, even by Satan himself. But when spiritual people sing a song, it becomes spiritual song.

Soul is the realm of Satan. He was cast out to the soul realm where he lives and operates and go to and fro. He is Beelzebub, the prince of the air. He attacks us from our soul being where sensual pleasure, intellect, emotions intellect are manipulated. It is the mind, a part of the heart, not the whole heart. We must worship the Lord with all our heart.

Being Under Satan's Yoke (BUSY)

The appearance of work looks satisfactory to a religious mind. Eve was so satisfied and enthused with the discovery of a new fellowship, and that she would be like God and would not die. At least she would do something practical and tangible.

She ate the forbidden fruit and she experienced just what the appearance of work look like to all people. She *"saw that the tree was good for food, and that it was a delight to the eyes, and that the tree was to be desired to make one wise, she took of the fruit thereof, and did eat; and she gave also unto her husband with her, and he did eat."* (Gen 3:6).

However, the result of that action was different from the confession.

"The eyes of them both were opened, and they knew that they were naked; and they sewed fig leaves together, and made themselves aprons. And they heard the voice of the LORD God walking in the garden in the cool of the day: and Adam and his wife hid themselves from the presence of the LORD God amongst the trees of the garden." (Gen 3:7-8).

That was the genesis of iniquity and eternal separation from God for Adam and Eve, and by extension the human race. That is the danger of prioritizing activities for God, rather than just loving Him. The latter looks too casual and uninvolving, unlike engaging in physical work – for God. But again, God is Spirit.

Satan is using the same as tool on earth, especially, in the last days. When we devote our *giftings* and graces to much activities for God rather than just to love, worship and obey Him, and allow Him to work His plans in us and through us, we are caught in Satan's plan to keep us busy. Someone defined BUSY as "Being Under Satan's Yoke". That has a semblance of truth is this context.

Love is the greatest commandment: to love the Lord your God with all your heart, not to work for the Lord your God with all your power. Much serving leads to weariness and to take offences, even against God. (Luke 10:40). Paul said:

> *"This one thing I do… I press toward the goal for the prize of the upward call of God in Christ Jesus. Therefore, let us, as many as are mature, have this mind; and if in anything you think otherwise, God shall reveal even this to you." (Php 3:13-15).*

When God brought Israel out of slavery in Egypt, His plan was to dwell with them in the camp. But when He came to do just that, they complained that His presence and glory was blinding. They requested that He would just speak to Moses, who would in turn, speak to them. They wanted something they could relate to, something they could see or feel, not so abstract or 'up there'. They made for themselves a golden calf and Aaron said to the people "This is your god, O Israel, that brought you out of the land of Egypt" (Exo 32:4).

Don't we all have a golden calf in our hearts? Our pulpits, altars, bibles, churches, ministries, works and even leaders!

Israel under Samuel also demanded God to give them a king so that they could be 'like other nations' around them. They were tired of God (who they couldn't see) being their King and Judge. They wanted a king that could be seen.

Samuel was very sad with that decision. It was an indictment on his person because Israel was rejecting his sons, who were sons of Belial. They did not *"walk in his ways; they turned aside after dishonest gain, took bribes, and perverted justice."* (1Sam 8:3). A case of a great prophet, but a weak father.

But the Lord said to Samuel: *"Heed the voice of the people in all that they say to you; fir they have not rejected you, but they have rejected Me, that I should not reign over them… however, you shall solemnly forewarn them, and show them the behavior of the king who will reign over them."* (1Sam 8:7-9).

Despite the warnings and the dangers of that request, and that they were rejecting God as King over them, preferring man rather than God, they were relentless. They got what they wanted and they paid for it.

Rejection always follows such a step. Lucifer, Adam and Eve, and every other examples in the scriptures were rejected by God for this reason.

Would He Spare Anyone?

Much has been said about iniquity. But worthy of note is a major characteristic of iniquity: it creeps in unsuspectingly. There is always a justification, encapsulated in ambition or desire to do or give something to God out of self effort.

This desire is particularly common in people or assemblies with means, zeal, or ability. Zeal eats up (Psa 69:9), zeal without knowledge. But when we abide in Him, we come into union with Him and we bear fruit for Him. He says:

"Abide in Me, and I in you. As the branch cannot bear fruit of itself, unless it abides in the vine; neither can you, except you abide in me." (John 15:4).

Who could be more gifted or endowed than Lucifer, the archangel and the commander of the host of heaven. But he desired more. The desire heightened to the point of rebellion and coveting the throne of God.

The same judgment on Lucifer, Adam and Eve, Cain and so on was given to the rich ruler, and indeed anyone who would not pay the price for relationship with Jesus. The rich ruler went out of Christ's presence because he could not pay the price. Jesus did not call him back. Nothing can be a substitute for relationship. What can we do without love?

The Garment

In the parable of the marriage feast, Jesus said a king made a marriage feast for His Son and called those He had invited to come for the feast. None of the invited guests honored the invitation. They gave various excuses why they couldn't come:

"One to his own farm, another to his business" – works. *"But when the king heard about it, he was furious. And he sent out his armies, destroyed those murderers, and burned up their city."* (Mat 22:5,7).

Knowing this, the king commanded His servants to go to the highways and byways and bring *"all whom they found, both bad and good: and the wedding hall was filled with guests."*

"But when the king came in to see the guests, he saw a man there who did not have on a wedding garment." (vs. 10-11). When he was asked how he ever got to the wedding, *"he was speechless. Then the king said to the servants, 'Bind him hand and foot, take him away, and cast him into outer darkness; there will be weeping and gnashing of teeth."* (Mat 22:12-13).

Even though the king invited everyone to the feast, he still required all to possess the only requirement to be in the feast – the wedding garment. That is the only thing that distinguishes the bride from the rest of the crowd. The wedding garment, among other things, shows that she is in love and in relationship with a special person whom she covenants to be with for the rest of her life.

We are also required, as believers to have a wedding garment to get to heaven, and Jesus is our garment. He is the righteousness of God. We must be clothed in His image and likeness, otherwise, we cannot be received to the marriage feast of the lamb.

If anyone is not clothed with Jesus, it is punishable to the fullest extent of His wrath. The gate of heaven will be bared to such.

Would He spare the last day believer who is not clothed in Christ's image? Would such people be welcomed as guests in the feast? Would they resemble anyone in heaven, even if they ever got there? When God sees us, He must see His Son in us. He must see the likeness of His Son in us. As the Father is, so also the Son, so must we be.

Before the throne of the Father, the bride is *"arrayed in a garment sprinkled with blood: and his name is called The Word of God… And he hath on his garment and on his thigh a name written, KING OF KINGS, AND LORD OF LORDS."* (Rev 19:13,16).

Book of Life

There are several books which contain the names of people qualified for rewards in heaven because of their works, labor and effort for God. It is the Book or Rewards, different from the Book of Life. It cannot bring people to heaven, but only reward those who get to heaven and have good works.

The Book of Life contains the names of those who are saved by grace alone, by faith alone, in Christ alone and by the word alone. It has nothing to do with works, efforts or labor.

Salvation is not by works, denominational affiliation, commitment, membership or religious affiliation.

"And anyone not found written in the book of life was cast into the lake of fire." (Rev 20:15).

We will only make heaven through relationship with Christ; being formed in His image and likeness.

Could a name exist in the book of rewards and not in the book of life? Could a name exist in the Book of Life and not in the book of reward? The answer to both question is probably yes. But one comes before the other.

We cannot be engaged in works for reward at the expense of grace for salvation and vice versa.

All our works, labor, efforts and sacrifice will be rewarded.

REPENT

"Remember therefore from where you have fallen; repent and do the first works, or else I will come to you quickly and remove your lampstand from its place – unless you repent." (Rev 2:5).

Our Filthy Rags

Ishmael was Abraham's works while Isaac was God's grace to him. God rejected all Abraham's appeal to let his works (Ishmael) live before Him, rather *"God said: 'No, Sarah your wife shall bear you a son, and you shall call his name Isaac; I will establish My covenant with him for an everlasting covenant, and with his descendants after him."* (Gen 17:18-19).

God did not reject Ishmael as a son, but as **the** son, He even blessed him (Gen 16:10). He asked Abraham to repent: he must send both the son, Ishmael and his mother, Hagar away. His works would not replace God's plan no matter how innocent (Gen 21:14).

Later, God gave the specification of the character of Abraham's work:

"He shall be a wild man; his hand shall be against every man, and every man's hand against him; and he shall dwell in the presence of all his brethren." (Gen 16:12).

That is what all our works looks like to God, filthy rags, at best.

Self Examination

At what point does our work become iniquity to God? At what point does our love begin to wax cold? When we are involved in much religious activity, it's time to watch it. It may bring good fruits, but while God is always good, good is not always God. God will be glorified in His plans, not our works (Eph 1:9).

Christianity is a spiritual working, not a charitable, religious or personal burden. It is about what He enables us to give Him, not what we can give Him.

Paul challenged the Corinthian assembly: *"Examine yourselves as to whether you are in the faith. Test yourselves. Do you not yourselves, how that Jesus Christ is in you? - unless you are disqualified."* (2Cor 13:5).

This is necessary so that we will not get to heaven and our works becomes iniquity before God which is very possible.

We can be so busy for God and at the end we are guilty before God. Our works may lead many to God, but we ourselves may be weighed down and crushed under the burden of the labor. We may spend time with the people of God and with the things of God, but not with God. Loving the things of God more than God is idolatry. It is time to repent.

When we spend less time with the scriptures, many times, to find sermon for the church in order to fulfill our duty as preachers, it is time to repent.

Bible reading must not replace Bible study. We must give our lives to God, not to people, to a course, church, ministry or even the best work of God; only to God. God is a 'jealous' God. He wants only Himself in us. If this is not the case, we must repent.

Fellowship with brethren is wonderful and we must desire it, regardless of personal differences (Heb 10:25). But we must understand that if we have fellowship with one another, up to sharing what we have, like the early church did, and even bound together with a common doctrine, and so on, if Christ is not in the center, it is as good as any religious meeting. In such meetings, music, prayer or other activities is the center. Emotion is replaced with the presence of the Holy Spirit. Songs of worship may be confused with worship itself.

Jesus told the woman at the well: *"The hour is coming, and now is, when the true worshippers will worship the Father in spirit and in truth; for the Father is seeking such to worship Him. God is Spirit, and those who worship Him must worship in spirit and truth."* (John 4:23-24).

Manifestations

Worshipping God is not in music, sermon, prayer or any of such wonderful things with cultural or doctrinal flavor. They may be good for outward expression, but not to be confused with presence of God.

Elijah was deceived when he saw the wind, earthquake and fire. He thought that was surely God's presence. But we read in 1Kng 19:11-12, *"but the LORD was not in the **wind**," "but the LORD was not in the **earthquake**," but the LORD was not in the **fire**." Although, the wind was "a great and strong wind rent the mountains, and brake in pieces the rocks before the LORD,"* but the Lord was not there, He came in a "still small voice."

How many of such great manifestations have we experienced in our meetings and we say "Surely, the presence of God is here?" Samuel made the same mistake when he saw Eliab. He looked on Eliab, and said, Surely the LORD'S anointed was before him.

"But the LORD said to Samuel, Do not look at his appearance or at his physical stature, because I have refused him. For the Lord does not see as a man sees; for man looks at the outward appearance, but the Lord looks at the heart." (1Sam 16:6-7).

Do we not make the same mistakes like these great prophets? Do we not judge things on outward appearances, manifestations and feelings? These are in the soul and are deceptive, so also our activities, labor and work. They are sometimes colored with culture or traditions to bring religious fulfillment. But God is Spirit and they that worship Him must worship Him in Spirit and in Truth.

Satan is the god of the soul realm, that is why soulish activities are not pleasing to God. Let us not look for activities, manifestations, signs and so on, but rather, let us be solid in God. Knowing Him may be without any great manifestation but a still small voice, unnoticed by the world. It will take a spiritual man to know that He is in God and God is in him. The things of the spirit are spirits.

While activities will definitely make us appear busy and active to the world, the secret of our fruitfulness here on earth and being with God in eternity is when we Abide in Him.

Paul acknowledged, gave thanks to God and prayed for the Thessalonian Church. The reason was their *"work of faith, labor of love, and patience of hope in the Lord Jesus Christ, in the sight of God and the Father."* (1Thes 1:2-3).

The Epistle

To the church at Ephesus, there was a work, labor and patience! The next verse revealed what these work of faith, labor of love and patience of hope in the Lord was: they *"were examples to all in Macedonia and Achaia who believe."* (1Thes 1:7). From them *"the word of the Lord has sounded forth, not only in Macedonia and Achaia, but also in every place your faith toward God has gone out, so that we need not to say anything."*

Their lives was the epistle that brought people in these cities and 'abroad' to God to the extent that Apostle Paul said they needed not to preach again. (1The 1:8).

Our lives must be the epistle that people read. Our exemplary lives must be the fragrance and irresistible aroma that compels people to come to Christ. Same Paul also told the Corinthian Church:

"Ye are our epistle written in our hearts, known and read by all men." (2Cor 3:2).

We must be more doers of the word than preachers of the word. We must preach the Gospel, if necessary, we may use words.

When we abide in Him, and He abides in us, greater fruits are produced for Him by Himself, using us only as emptying vessels. Such works are the works of faith, greater than when we hold crusade to host millions of people.

We may run around trying to save the lost, but He has not asked us to save them, He asks us to simply tell them about Him and He would do the rest. We cannot bring anyone to Christ; we couldn't even come to Christ on our own, how then could we bring others to Him? Jesus said:

"No man can come to Me, unless it has been granted to him by My Father." (Joh 6:65). *"The message of the cross is foolishness to those who are perishing; but to us who are being saved it is the power of God."* (1Cor 1:18).

It is Christ that brings people to Himself, not we Christ's 'strategy' is discipleship, not conversion.

"Go therefore and make disciples of all the nations, baptizing them into the name of the Father and of the Son and of the Holy Spirit, teaching them to observe all things that I commanded you; and lo, I am with you always, even unto the end of the age." (Mat 28:19-20).

Time Up

It is time to repent from works and press into the love of God which He gave us, which is Christ. It is only the love He gave to us that can save us; all other things will attract His wrath.

When activities in the church gives us joy more than being alone with God or when we have more of a corporate than a personal prayer life, it's time to repent.

The Church is a family of God, a household of faith and we are all brothers and sisters of one family. But when our gathering is more of looking for solutions to our problems, it is time to repent.

When we always desire someone to pray for us and we no longer hear the voice of God, or when the word of God is not the most elevated in our lives, it is time to repent.

When we move more by burden than by leading or when we no longer respond to the Holy Spirit's conviction, or we struggle with sin more than to obey God, it is time to repent. When people tell us how wonderful our ministry is and how abundant the fruits of our labor in the kingdom is, it is time to watch it.

God is looking for His love (Jesus) in us, not His work in us. Paul said without love, even if he spoke with the tongues of men and of angels, he would be like a sounding brass, or a tinkling cymbal. If he had the gift of prophecy, and understood all mysteries, and all knowledge; and had all faith, so that he could remove mountains, he was nothing. And though he gave all had to feed the poor, and gave his body to be burned, it did not profit him (1Cor 13:1-3).

In an earlier chapter, he said:

"But I discipline my body and bring it into subjection, lest, when I have preached to others, I myself should become disqualified." (1Cor 9:27).

If that was a possibility with Paul, it is with us, too.

We must be Mary, not Martha. Martha expended much effort in trying to prepare a meal for Jesus (works), but Mary sat at Jesus' feet to know Him (relationship). Martha asked Jesus to persuade Mary to join her in the great works and labor she was involved in for the Lord. Jesus commended her labor, but said she was too burdened with many works and activities, trying to please the Master. But the

Master is more interested in us knowing Him and He, knowing us. He said Mary had chosen that and it would not be taken away from her. (Luke 10:40-42).

The call to each of the disciples is:

"Follow me and I will make you..." (Mat 4:19; Mark 1:17).

It is not we that make ourselves; not Bible school, doctrine, people, etc, He makes us WHEN we follow Him, not when we do great things for Him. As we follow Him, He makes us to work what is pleasing to Him. He only needs our availability, not ability.

People can make us anything and confer on us ministerial titles, but only Christ conforms us to His image.

The sad news is that much effort is expended on works, activities and programs by many individuals, churches, religious organizations and ministries. For many of these, there remains no more oil in the lamp to light the path to see *"what is good; and what does the LORD require of you."* (Mic 6:8).

For this reason, Jesus rebuked the Pharisees. He called them blind and hypocrites. They *"pay tithe of mint and anise and cummin, and have neglected the weightier matters of the law: justice and mercy and faith. These you ought to have done, without leaving the other undone. Blind guides… you cleanse the outside of the cup and dish, but inside they are full of extortion and self-indulgence."* (Mat 23:23-35).

We concentrate on making the outside clean at the detriment of the inside. We concentrate on works at the expense of relationship.

While our works may earn us respect here on earth and a crown in heaven, it will not be the yardstick to making heaven. It is better settled here on earth. Eternity is too costly to discover if Jesus know us or not. There must be repentance now, because the night comes when no one works again and there is nowhere to buy oil. The shout of the arrival of the bridegroom is near.

How will you deal with Christ's words: *'I know your works'?* He sees and acknowledges your personal works, labor and effort for Him or in your assembly, but He wants more than that, He wants relationship. How is your relationship with Him? Is it strong enough to produce His image and likeness in you? When you stand before God, will Christ be there to say He knows you or will you depend on your works to save you? By works shall no flesh be justified before Him. Christ (not works) in us, is the hope of Glory (Col 1:27).

He who has ears, let him hear what the Spirit says to the churches.

ABOUT THE AUTHOR

'Bola Olu-Jordan is a prophetic teacher with an early church apostolic imprint. He has a deep insight into spirituality and his works often reflect non-religious but divine approach to faith. His passion for Missions and Discipleship has opened doors of fellowship around the world. He is the publisher CRYOUT Magazine. He has authored many books among which are *The Great Possession*, *What God Forgot To Say*, *Capsules of Faith* and *The Mystery of Union in Marriage*.

Author contacts:
Facebook Page: www.facebook.com/bolaolujordan
Twitter: www.twitter.com/Pastorj0rdan

CRYOUT Publications accepts Christian manuscripts for both POD and E-Book Publishing.
For quotes on complete pre-press services, including formatting, editing, graphics and printing, and list of published works, please visit cryoutreach.com

.